Letters TO Zachary

This book is dedicated to four amazing people. First, to the Lord Almighty who, in His infinite wisdom, gave me the perfect son and gave me the tools to be able to take care of the Earthly angel that was my son. Second, to my son who was always a joy, very laid back, never met a stranger, and made any room that he entered better just by his mere presence. Third, to my wife who always gave our beloved son the most free flowing love, support, and care his entire life. Fourth and finally, to my parents who loved, accepted their grandson with all of his disabilities, and always gave 100% unconditional love to him from Day 1.

Zachary loved to the fullest, laughed the hardest, and never let anything get him down. He faced all challenges head on with a smile on his face. Zachary taught me what life was all about. My son LOVED weather and The Weather Channel. He also LOVED the ladies (blondes specifically).

Jason Tuttle, Zachary's dad,& Creator of Letters To Zachary. LettersToZachary.com

...the moment is all we have.

Zach was always happy and smiling. He was always living in the now - not the past nor in the future. He taught me that the moment is all that we have. I'll never forget that... It did not matter that Zach had multiple disabilities. He was always a happy, loving child that never complained. His smile and hugs were contagious!!

Mike Tuttle, Sharpsburg GA
Zachary's granddad

Forever Happy and Always Smiling

Whenever I entered his home, Z-Man (as I often called him) would immediately clap, squeal, smile, and laugh. I always bowed like a Queen when this ovation occurred. I will forever remember him doing this.

Cheryl T, Grandmother to Z
Sharpsburg GA. USA

Samantha and Zachary shared a loving brother-sister bond and had their own nonverbal communication. Samantha loved anything her brother did (i.e. riding the school bus, swimming, The Weather Channel, horseback riding, therapy, and Special Olympics bowling).

Samantha Tuttle
Zachary's Little Sister
LettersToZachary.com

"Being a parent who has lost a child is like trying to understand how to properly fold a fitted sheet. No one knows how to do it."

Being a parent who has lost a child is like trying to understand how to properly fold a fitted sheet. No one knows how to do it.

-Jason Tuttle

The irony of silence is that it's supposed to be quiet but in the life of a griever it is deafening.

The irony of silence is that it's supposed to be quiet but in the life of a griever it is deafening.

-Jason Tuttle

It's okay to need someone to talk to or just sit with someone in silence.

-Jason Tuttle

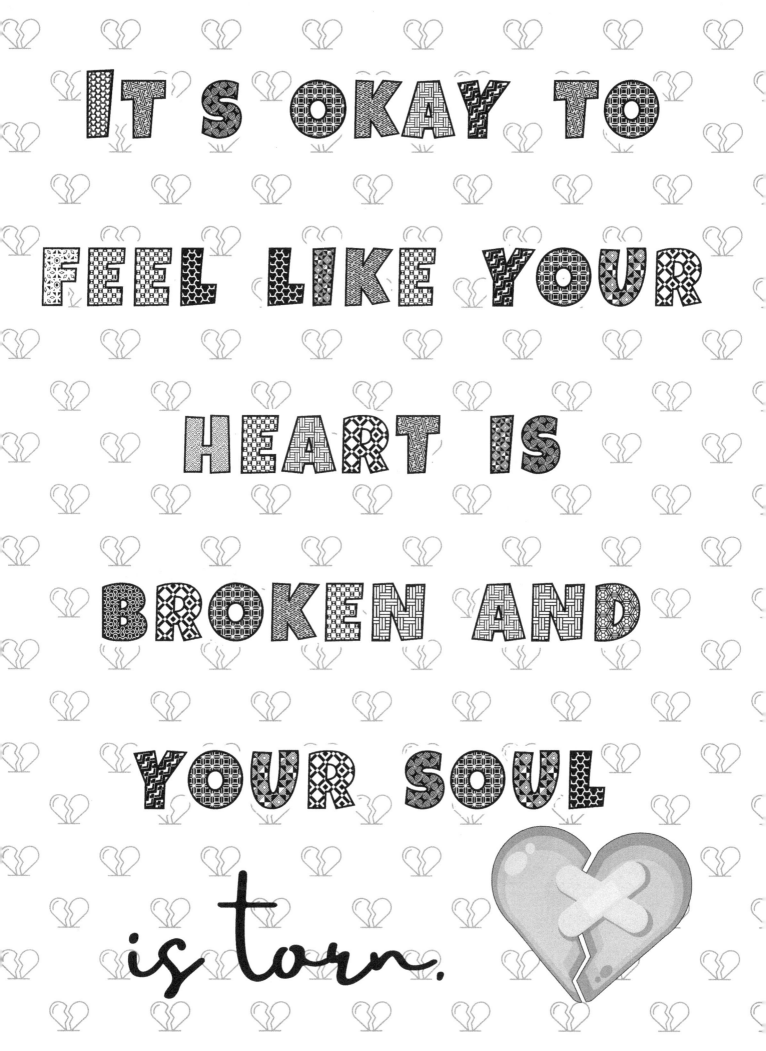

IT'S OKAY TO FEEL LIKE YOUR HEART IS BROKEN AND YOUR SOUL is torn.

It's okay to feel like your heart is broken and your soul is torn.

-Jason Tuttle

Tanner was a national champion at shotput and discus throwing. He was the one to beat. He came to every meet with determination to beat his last personal record. Tanner was well respected, loving, kind and a gentle giant. He is missed dearly by his mama.
I love you, D.
You are forever in my heart.

Holly D. - Brookhaven, Georgia, USA

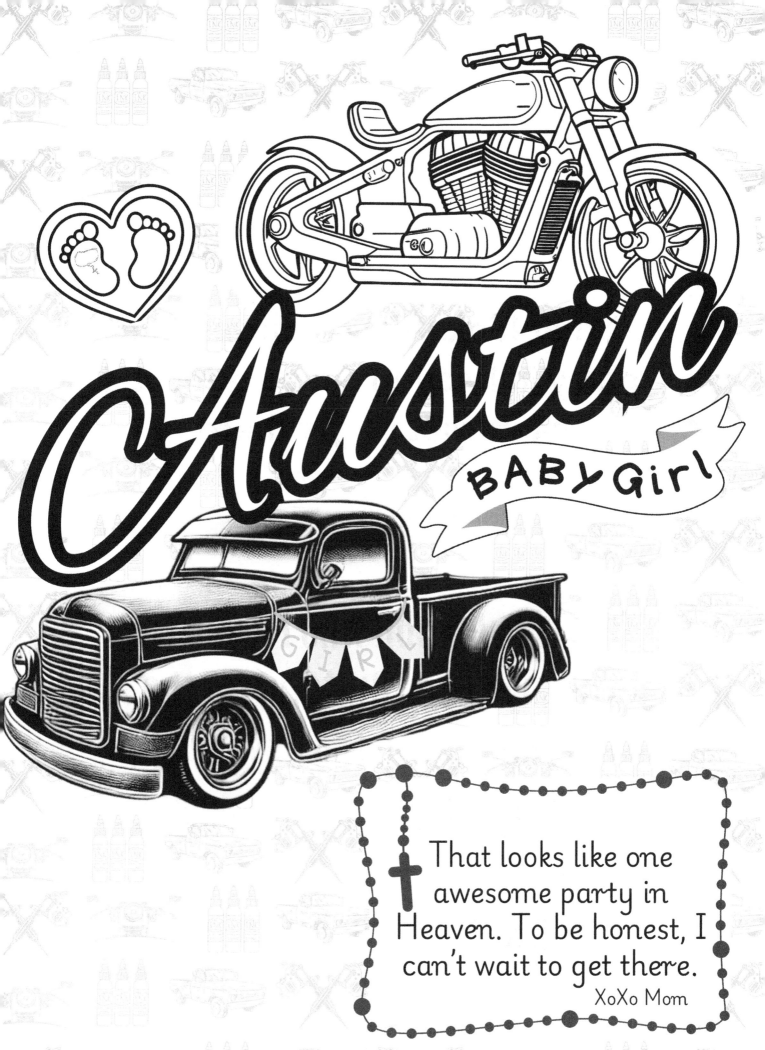

Austin

BABY Girl

That looks like one awesome party in Heaven. To be honest, I can't wait to get there.

XoXo Mom

"That looks like one awesome party in Heaven. To be honest, I can't wait to get there."

This is to my son who I loved with all my heart. Grateful for the words spoken on the days leading to you going to be with Jesus.

Paula H.-North Richland TX. USA

"The strongest, bravest, most courageous person I've ever known."

In honor of my precious daughter, Rachel Sweet. I was your sole caregiver. You were my SOUL caregiver. You taught me more than I taught you. I needed you more than you needed me.

Stacey S-M.-Lincoln, MA U.S.A.

Live Like Lambuth

Lambuth
loved God,
his family,
his church,
and reading his Bible.
He would want you
to make it to Heaven.

#LiveLikeLambuth

#livelikelambuth

My hero transitioned from his earthly flesh to his glorious heavenly home, to be with his Savior forever. We are temporarily separated until we are joined together. My wish for you is that you would live as my hero did, #livelikelambuth.

Melanie Wallace
Centreville, AL

DANIEL

THIS IS THE BEST DAY EVER

My son Daniel loved to say "This is the best day ever!" Now that he is gone I try to make sure every day is the best day ever!

Daniel, I will love you until I can hug you again.

Cathy N.- Phoenix, AZ

"Every day I wake up brings me one day closer to seeing you again."

Deeply missing my "Zach hugs" and our adventures. Can't wait to see your smile and hear your laugh again. I want to tell you of all the places all over the world our Zach Music rocks have travelled to.
I love you Z 🎶 -Mom

Jill Music Frew

When it rains you are crying with me.

Zachery "Jake," you loved the water and I remember how much you would say you wanted to live close to the Frio. You saw the good in everyone and I remember one time you asking me why people took advantage of that. I will continue to see the good in people just as you did, my sunshine. Love always, mom.

Michelle G.-Pleasanton, TX
(Check the co-ordinates on the page)

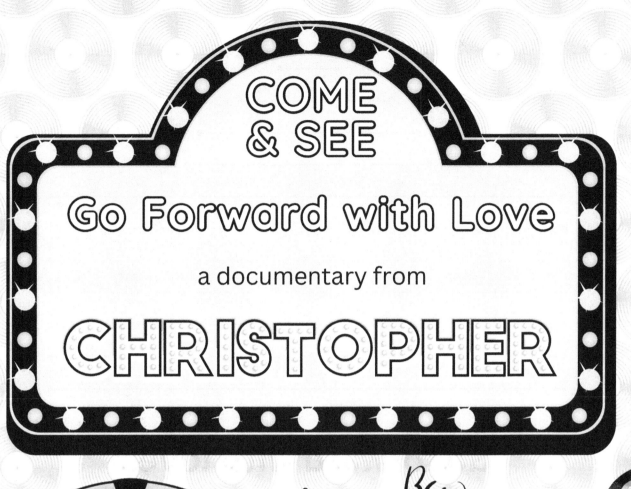

COME & SEE

Go Forward with Love

a documentary from

CHRISTOPHER

...Buttercup...

The reviews are in...

☆☆☆☆☆
You'll Sing , You'll Dance
The story is short, but liked by so many.

☆☆☆☆☆
Heart of my Heart
Story leaves you with cherished memories.

☆☆☆☆☆
Change the world
This story will help so many.

"Go forward with love."

Heart of my Heart.

Robin J.-Independence, MO

"You've become a part of nature's beauty."

My son, Zak enjoyed kayaking and canoeing. He felt at one with nature when he was on the water. His ashes dispersed in the estuary becoming a part of this natural beauty.

Linda W.-Fareham, Hampshire, UK

I love you to the moon and back.

Nickki, forever 24. Forever my
little Budda XO

I miss you so much, XO Mom

Amy Jo L.-New Orleans, LA

"Loyalty Over Love."

My Brendan only lived a short 20 years - a life so brief yet so beautiful. I called him Baby Brown Eyes because he had the most beautiful, big brown eyes. As he got older he would get a huge smile on his face when I called him that.
I miss him so much!

Lisa H.-Bridgeton, MO. USA

Sunset Stories Podcast, where we tell the stories of our loved ones. Our motto is 'Let's heal together.'

This is dedicated to my sons Easton and CJ, both in Heaven.

Tanya Manley, Sunset Stories Podcast
Dallas, TX

These broken wings have kept me falling

I am running, pain is calling

And while I try to get by safely

My broken heart says, "Make it hasty"

So I run faster, but soon I crash

And forty years wet my lash

The light goes out– it's time to sleep

I hope I know my soul you'll keep.

~Rhiannon Hennessey

"These broken wings have kept me falling/ I am running, pain is calling/ And while I try to get by safely/ My broken heart says, "Make it hasty" /So I run faster, but soon I crash/ And forty years wet my lash/ The light goes out - it's time to sleep/ I hope I know my soul you'll keep."
-Rhiannon Hennessey

My beautiful daughter, Rhiannon, crossed over 2-20-23. She is a bright light. She is a talented artist, writer, creator, and a beautiful soul.

Dawn H.

I'm Okay.

My youngest boy Devin used to always say "I'm okay." After his passing, this is something that runs through my mind. I know that though it's sad he is gone, he's okay now.

Lenny H.-Middleton, ID

Too Soon

Anytime that you left before me would have been too soon, but this too soon was too soon, too soon, too soon.

To my Crys - we will continue to carry your legacy in our hearts forever. You brought joy to so very many people.

My daughter loved dandelions.

Debra M.- Burleson, TX. USA

Logan will always be remembered as a generous, caring person who loved cats and funny t-shirts.

Logan loved to bake chocolate chip cookies and share them with others. He wanted to save the world.

He left behind his parents, brother, and sister who will miss him forever.

Kandace K.-West Linn, OR. USA

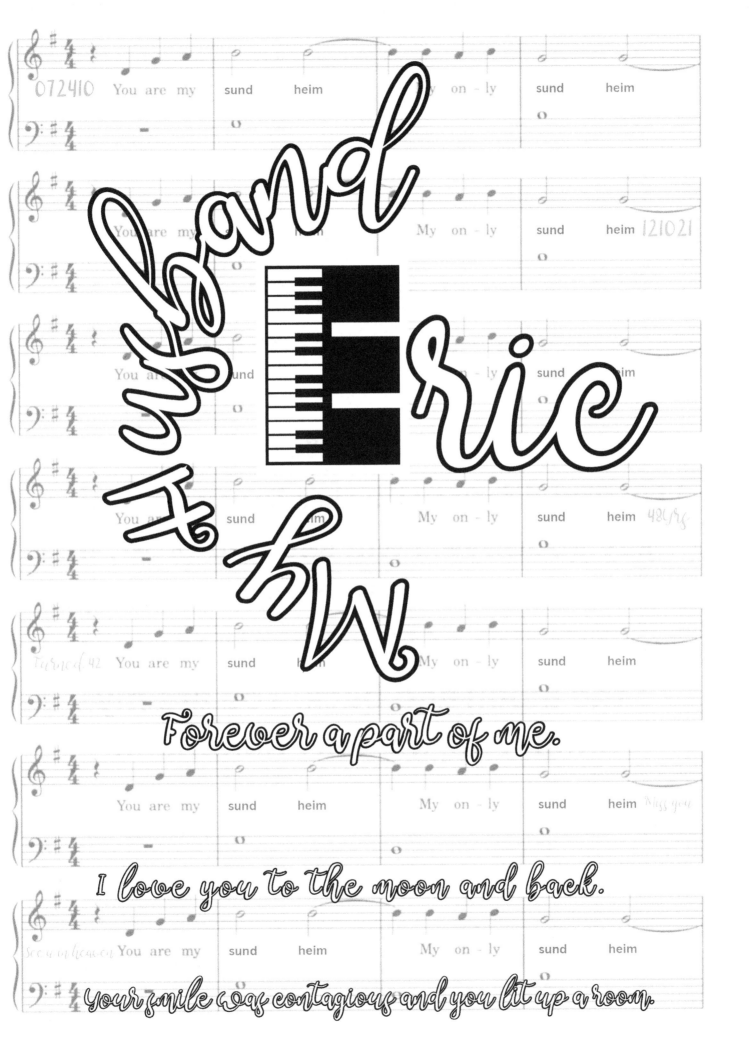

My husband Eric.
Forever a part of me.

You left this world before I was ready. I turned 42 just the day before I had to say goodbye. I will see you later, in our eternal home, but I really miss you on this side of Heaven. I love you to the moon and back. You are my "Sundheim, my only Sundheim."

Jennifer S.-Willmar, MN

Tanner's Vibe

Tanner was always dancing and playing his guitar. He was killed by a drunk driver.
Don't drink and drive!

Tanner loved snow, his cat Clansy, playing guitar, traveling, dancing and spreading good and happy vibes!

Renee L.- Denver, CO

Redneck

My son was one of the biggest rednecks there was. He was born in Alabama, moved to Texas when he was 23. He loved everything about America and what the flag stood for. I love and miss him so very much.

Hope J.-United States

Create joy and dance. Dallin was adventurous and he loved water and to be on fast boats.

To my muse, the one who brought joy and continues to share the music so we will dance... forever and eternity. The Boy Who Became More Then We Could Imagine (Memoir dedicate to Dallin).

The Boy Who Became More Than We Could Imagine

Julia P.-Utah. Always Dallin's Mom

"You made the best decision you could with the information you had at the time and every decision was carefully made with love."

My son Georgie was born premature with congenital heart disease but he was so much more than his medical issues. He died right before his second birthday. In his short life he taught me how to find joy and wonder in everyday things. He was just so happy to be alive and had a special connection with animals, especially our chunky beagle Monty.

Victoria R.-Chesterfield, VA

"Without Speaking a Word"

My little brother, Matthew, passed away at age 12. He never spoke a word but the impact he made on my life was more powerful than any word that could ever be spoken. His legacy lives on! He loved when I would play the piano in his room. Sometimes it would make him laugh. A summer camp and respite program was started in his memory and continues to serve many kids and youth with special needs.

Karen J
-Newnan, Georgia, USA

Grief

simply

but

is

Love

with

no place to go.

"Grief, simply put, is love with no place to go."

Grieving is a painful journey, one best not taken alone. Contrary to some perceptions, the process of grieving after the death of a loved one is not a simple step by step process. Nor is it the same for everyone.

It's time for grief to come out of the basement or wherever we have stuffed it to avoid talking about it. The only way we can continue to put one foot in front of the other while living and grieving at the same time is to be able to talk about our memories, be honest about our feelings and support others that are walking a similar path. Less isolation, more community. We hope you will join us.

Listen to our podcast, <u>As I Live and Grieve</u>, available through your favorite app.

As I Live and Grieve Podcast, Kathy Gleason-Rochester, NY

Mom

You always told me that this too "honey," will pass. That sad times don't always last. I look in the mirror and see you looking back at me. I see you in the eyes of my children and this brings me comfort. I hear your voice in the wind, and I feel your spirit in every beat of my heart.

I felt everything stop and it was if I was walking in slow motion when I realized that you were gone. I remember it like it was yesterday as I felt the impact of a life without you, and my body crumpled to the floor. I prayed with all my might that you would hear me and protect my unborn baby. It was in that moment of reflection that I felt your presence and I knew my baby would be safe. He came early and I know his birth happened right when we needed hope the most. I still pray to you, and tell you funny stories, and pour out my words in my heart onto the page. I know you see me, feel my love for you. I will miss you forever and always, my beloved mama, Betty.

Jeanine L.-Saskatchewan, Canada
Creator of the blog and podcast
House of a Writer

You are loved and a blessing.

Mary C.- USA
Zac's Great Aunt

I watched my Dad suffer and change as his stage 4 lung cancer metastasized throughout his body. He lost his physical strength, independence, pride, and, worst of all, his sense of humor and love. For him, his passing was a welcomed release.

Karen M-Randolph, MA

Andrea,

our love has no measure. Our eternal love is a shining light that guides me to hope for tomorrow. I feel you in the breeze, I hear you in silence, I see you in the sun, moon. and stars. I walk this life with you beside me.

Love is forever.

"Andrea, our love has no measure. Our eternal love is a shining light that guides me to hope for tomorrow. I feel you in the breeze, I hear you in silence, I see you in the sun, moon, and stars. I walk this life with you beside me. Love is forever."

Andrea, the echo of your quiet giggles and your sweet soft voice are forever in my mind. From birth you imprinted your presence in my heart forever. My child, my treasure, and my gift from God.

Linda Henderson Trenton, Ontario, Canada

Thank You

Grief is a collective event that is experienced individually. However, since the beginning of my grief journey, I have several people to whom I owe a huge Thank You.

My wife, who has been 100% supportive throughout this entire journey, "Sunset Stories" podcast with Tanya Manley, "Grief 2 Hope" online grief sessions with Hope Reger, "Grief 101" YouTube series with Lenny Hunt, "Grief Let's Talk About It" podcast with Tony Lynch, "Release Grief" podcast with Faith Sage. "Our Dead Dads" podcast with Nick Gaylord, "The Price of Love" online grief sessions with Paula Bloom Hill, and a multitude of others. It certainly takes a village and a village that I am forever grateful for all of their support.

-Jason Tuttle

Zachary's Dad
LettersToZachary.com

Find Us!

LettersToZachary.com

Linktree

Grief Community Facebook Group

Instagram

Made in the USA
Coppell, TX
16 August 2024

36081882R10044